DEADLY BITERS

GRIZZLY BEARS BITE!

BY JANEY LEVY

Gareth Stevens
PUBLISHING

Please visit our website, www.garethstevens.com. For a free color catalog of all our high-quality books, call toll free 1-800-542-2595 or fax 1-877-542-2596.

Cataloging-in-Publication Data

Names: Levy, Janey.
Title: Grizzly bears bite! / Janey Levy.
Description: New York : Gareth Stevens Publishing, 2021. | Series: Deadly biters | Includes glossary and index.
Identifiers: ISBN 9781538257708 (pbk.) | ISBN 9781538257722 (library bound) | ISBN 9781538257715 (6 pack)
Subjects: LCSH: Grizzly bear--Juvenile literature.
Classification: LCC QL737.C27 L48 2021 | DDC 599.784--dc23

First Edition

Published in 2021 by
Gareth Stevens Publishing
111 East 14th Street, Suite 349
New York, NY 10003

Copyright © 2021 Gareth Stevens Publishing

Designer: Reann Nye
Editor: Meta Manchester

Photo credits: Cover, p. 1 Scott E Read/Shutterstock.com; cover, pp. 1-24 (background) Reinhold Leitner/Shutterstock.com; p. 5 Laura Hedien/Moment/Getty Images; p. 6 Daria Rybakova/Shutterstock.com; p. 7 Ad_hominem/Shutterstock.com; p. 9 Mike Korostelev www.mkorostelev.com/Moment/Getty Images; p. 10 Jack Nevitt/Shutterstock.com; p. 11 Aaron/Moment/Getty Images; p. 13 critterbiz/Shutterstock.com; p. 14 unive/Shutterstock.com; p. 15 knelson20/Shutterstock.com; p. 16 Egor Vlasov/Shutterstock.com; p. 17 by wildestanimal/Moment/Getty Images; p. 19 Joe McDonald/The Image Bank/Getty Images; p. 21 Paul Souders/Stone/Getty Images.

Printed in the United States of America

Some of the images in this book illustrate individuals who are models. The depictions do not imply actual situations or events.

CPSIA compliance information: Batch #CS20GS: For further information contact Gareth Stevens, New York, New York at 1-800-542-2595.

Find us on

CONTENTS

Words in the glossary appear in **bold** type
the first time they are used in the text.

GREET THE GRIZZLY BEAR

Maybe you've seen grizzly bears at a zoo. They're a type of brown bear. They're called "grizzly bears" because the tips of their fur are grizzled, which means they're gray, silver, or white.

Grizzly bears eat mostly plants. But these animals aren't teddy bears. They also eat meat. And they're huge, powerful creatures that can kill animals as large as moose, helped by their sharp teeth and strong bite. You'll learn lots more about grizzlies and their bite inside this book.

CHEW ON THIS!

One kind of grizzly bear's scientific name is *Ursus arctos horribilis*. That means horrible northern bear!

Grizzlies can live about 25 years in the wild.

GRIZZLY BEARS' HOMES

If you want to see grizzly bears in the wild, you won't have to travel far. These bears live in North America. The largest numbers of grizzlies are found in northern and western Canada and in Alaska. But some also live in Idaho, Montana, Washington state, and Wyoming.

Grizzlies are able to live in many kinds of **habitats**. They live in woodlands, forests, meadows, mountains, and **prairies**. They often choose to live along rivers and streams.

CHEW ON THIS!

Grizzly bears came to North America from Asia sometime between 50,000 and 25,000 years ago.

GRIZZLIES IN NORTH AMERICA

ALASKA

CANADA

■ GRIZZLY BEAR TERRITORY

UNITED STATES

You can see grizzlies in the wild in these places,
but you should never get too close to them!

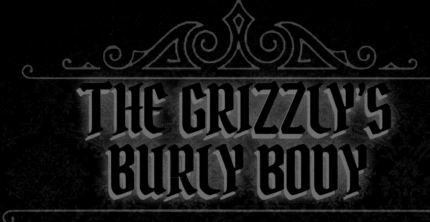

THE GRIZZLY'S BURLY BODY

How can you tell if a bear is a grizzly? Its fur—usually dark brown—has lighter-colored grizzled tips. Unlike other bears, it has a large hump on its shoulders. It has long legs, a large head with a dish-shaped face, and a long **snout**.

Male grizzlies are huge. They can be over 8 feet (2.4 m) long and weigh over 800 pounds (363 kg). They can be 4 feet (1.2 m) tall at the shoulder. Female grizzlies are smaller.

CHEW ON THIS!

Grizzlies see about as well as people, but they have a very good sense of hearing and a great sense of smell. Their sense of smell is mainly what helps them understand the world around them.

Grizzlies have claws up to 5 inches (13 cm) long on their front feet! They use these for digging up food, catching fish, and digging dens for winter.

CLAWS

AWESOME OMNIVORES

Grizzlies are powerful predators. Some people might think of these giant animals as carnivores, or meat eaters. But the truth is that grizzlies are **omnivores**.

Yes, grizzlies eat meat. They hunt elk, deer, and moose. They catch fish—they mainly like salmon. They eat **rodents** such as squirrels. They'll also scavenge, or eat animals that are already dead. But you might be surprised to learn that plants make up three-fourths of what they eat. They dine on roots, grasses, fruits, berries, and nuts.

CHEW ON THIS!

Grizzlies may hide food in holes to come back to later. They also eat food that people have thrown away.

When salmon travel up Alaskan rivers to lay
their eggs, grizzlies gather to catch them.

A BRUTAL BITE

When grizzlies need to chomp down hard on **prey**, they have the bite for it. Their bite force is about 1,200 pounds per square inch (84.4 kg per sq cm). That's stronger than the bite force of mighty predators such as the lion and tiger!

Their huge head and strong **muscles** in their **jaws** make their bite so powerful. And they have some sharp teeth in the front of their mouth that make the bite even worse.

CHEW ON THIS!

Do you want to compare your bite force to a grizzly's? An adult man's bite force, which is stronger than yours, is only 174 pounds per square inch (12.2 kg per sq cm)!

The long teeth in the grizzly's mouth are called canines. The small teeth between the canines in the front of the mouth are called incisors.

JAW

TEETH

MOUTH

CYCLE OF THE SEASONS

The seasons of the year have a strong effect on a grizzly's life. In spring and early summer, grizzlies eat and look for **mates**. They keep eating and eating during summer and early fall to gain weight. They'll need that weight for winter.

As the weather becomes colder and food starts to disappear, grizzlies dig dens for winter. They'll spend the winter **hibernating** in those dens and living off their fat. Females even have their cubs while they're hibernating!

CHEW ON THIS!

While grizzlies are hibernating, their heartbeat slows down from about 80 beats per minute to just about 18 beats per minute. They also don't go to the bathroom at all while they hibernate!

This gives you a good idea of how hugely fat grizzlies get to prepare for winter hibernation! They can gain up to about 3 pounds (1.4 kg) per day!

CARING FOR CUBS

Mother grizzlies usually have two cubs. The cubs are tiny—they weigh less than a pound (453.6 g)! When they're born, cubs are blind and have no fur or teeth. They nurse from their mother and grow strong. When spring comes, the family leaves the den.

Cubs stay with their mother for two to three years. She teaches them what they need to know to survive. She also keeps them safe. She'll attack anything she thinks puts her cubs in danger!

CHEW ON THIS!

Sadly, almost half of cubs die during their first year due to sickness, hunger, and predators such as wolves and mountain lions. Even adult male grizzlies kill cubs!

Just like human children, grizzly cubs have a lot to learn before they're ready to go out on their own.

GRIZZLIES AND PEOPLE

Do grizzlies ever attack people? They do sometimes. Attacks are most likely if people surprise grizzlies, come upon a mother with cubs, or find a grizzly eating a dead animal. But people have also harmed grizzlies.

Grizzlies once lived all over western North America. Native Americans have many tales about them. Grizzlies lost most of their habitat as European settlers moved in and killed them out of fear. Now, only around 1,000 grizzlies live south of Canada.

CHEW ON THIS!

In Canada, where there are lots of grizzlies, hunters go after the bears as big game trophies, or prizes. However, in 2017, it was outlawed in British Columbia.

People can go on tours to take pictures of grizzlies in the wild. Knowing about grizzlies can help people get great shots!

A FUTURE FOR GRIZZLIES

What will happen to grizzlies? No one knows for sure. But grizzlies in the United States outside of Alaska are now **protected** by law. That means it's against the law for people to kill them.

There are also groups working to protect grizzly bear habitats to make sure grizzlies have the kind of places they need to live healthy lives. These groups are also trying to reduce problems between grizzlies and people. They want people to learn how to live with grizzlies in peace.

CHEW ON THIS!

To keep grizzlies safe, it's important to keep them from getting comfortable being around people. Never feed them and keep trash stored in objects the grizzlies can't open.

One wildlife group called the National Wildlife Federation is trying to bring grizzlies back to places where they used to live.

GLOSSARY

habitat: the natural place where an animal or plant lives

hibernate: to be in a sleeplike state for a long period of time, usually during the winter

jaws: the bones that hold the teeth and make up the mouth

mate: one of two animals that come together to produce babies

muscle: one of the parts of the body that allow movement

omnivore: an animal that eats both meat and plants

prairie: a large, mostly flat area of land in North America that is covered in grass and has few trees

prey: an animal that is hunted by other animals for food

protect: to keep safe

rodent: a small, furry animal with large front teeth, such as a mouse or rat

snout: an animal's nose and mouth

FOR MORE INFORMATION

BOOKS

Carney, Elizabeth. *Bears*. Washington, DC: National Geographic Partners, 2016.

Emminizer, Theresa. *Grizzly Bears*. New York, NY: PowerKids Press, 2019.

Poole, H. W. *Grizzly Bears*. New York, NY: Children's Press, 2019.

WEBSITES

Brown Bear
kids.nationalgeographic.com/animals/mammals/brown-bear/
Learn more about grizzly bears and watch a video of a grizzly bear's meal.

San Diego Zoo Kids: Brown Bear
kids.sandiegozoo.org/animals/brown-bear
Discover more about grizzlies and other brown bears on this site—and even hear one roar!

The Good, the Bad, and the Grizzly: What to Do If You Encounter a Bear
www.pbs.org/wnet/nature/the-good-the-bad-and-the-grizzly-what-to-do-if-you-encounter-a-bear/117/
Learn how to stay safe if you have a surprise meeting with a grizzly.

INDEX